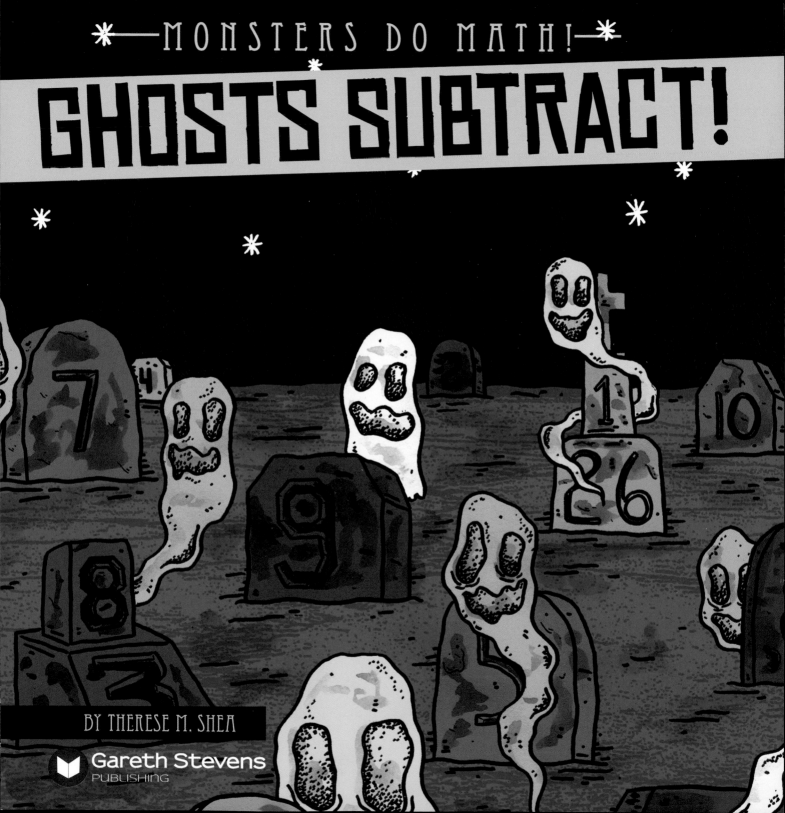

Please visit our website, www.garethstevens.com. For a free color catalog of all
our high-quality books, call toll free 1-800-542-2595 or fax 1-877-542-2596.

Cataloging-in-Publication Data

Names: Shea, Therese M.
Title: Ghosts subtract! / Therese M. Shea.
Description: New York : Gareth Stevens Publishing, 2019. | Series: Monsters do
math! | Includes glossary and index.
Identifiers: LCCN ISBN 9781538232965 (pbk.) | ISBN 9781538229330 (library bound) |
ISBN 9781538232972 (6 pack)
Subjects: LCSH: Subtraction--Juvenile literature. | Arithmetic--Juvenile
literature. | Ghosts--Juvenile literature.
Classification: LCC QA115.S54 2019 | DDC 513.2'12--dc23

First Edition

Published in 2019 by
Gareth Stevens Publishing
111 East 14th Street, Suite 349
New York, NY 10003

Designer: Sarah Liddell
Editor: Kate Light
Illustrator: Bobby Griffiths

Photo credits: p. 4 Lemon Tree Images/Shutterstock.com; p. 5 Tom Tom/
Shutterstock.com; p. 6 Ilkin Zeferli/Shutterstock.com; p. 9 Kobby Dagan/
Shutterstock.com; p. 10 korkeng/Shutterstock.com; p. 13 Aleksei Isachenko/
Shutterstock.com; p. 15 Dariusz Majgier/Shutterstock.com; p. 17 Kean Collection/
Staff/Archive Photos/Getty Images; p. 19 Co9man/Wikimedia Commons;
p. 20 andreiuc88/Shutterstock.com; p. 21 Alexander Ishchenko/Shutterstock.com.

Printed in the United States of America

CPSIA compliance information: Batch #CW19GS: For further information contact Gareth Stevens, New York, New York at 1-800-542-2595.

CONTENTS

Words in the glossary appear in **bold** type the first time they are used in the text.

DON'T BE AFRAID!

Do you love ghost stories? Some tales are about ghosts that are **invisible.** Other ghosts look like people, but are see-through. Still others look like they're wearing white sheets!

Do you believe in ghosts? You'll want to believe in the ghosts in this book. They're helpful spirits! They'll help you figure out some kinds of subtraction problems. You can check your answers in the answer key on page 22. So, turn the page. These friendly ghosts aren't scary. They're just smart—scary smart!

4

THERE ARE OTHER NAMES FOR GHOSTS. SOMETIMES
THEY'RE CALLED BOGEYS, PHANTOMS, SPECTERS, OR SPIRITS!

HAUNTED WORD PROBLEMS

Ghosts are great at word problems. In fact, ghosts can help you set up an **equation** and find the answer! But if no ghosts are handy, you can use pictures of ghosts to **represent** the numbers in an equation.

MONSTER FACTS!
GHOSTS ARE SAID TO MOVE OBJECTS AND MAKE STRANGE LIGHTS APPEAR.

There are 15 ghosts in a haunted house. Five of those ghosts think it's too crowded. They move next door! How many ghosts are left in the first haunted house? Use the picture to help you set up and **solve** an equation.

? ghosts – ? ghosts = ? ghosts

There are 11 ghosts haunting a **graveyard.** One ghost gets scared. It goes home and hides! Then, two other ghosts leave to visit a haunted house. How many ghosts are left in the graveyard? Use the picture to help you set up and solve an equation.

? ghosts – ? ghost – ? ghosts = ? ghosts

MONSTER FACTS!
SOME PEOPLE AROUND THE WORLD HOLD CELEBRATIONS
IN GRAVEYARDS TO HONOR THEIR DEAD. IN MEXICO, PEOPLE
CELEBRATE DÍA DE LOS MUERTOS—THE DAY OF THE DEAD!

Putting objects in groups of 10 can help you solve a subtraction problem even faster. Luckily, some ghosts like to play games in groups of 10!

MONSTER FACTS!
SOME PEOPLE BELIEVE GHOSTS MAKE NOISE. THEY SAY THEY'VE HEARD GHOSTLY LAUGHTER. SCREAMS. FOOTSTEPS. AND RINGING BELLS!

10

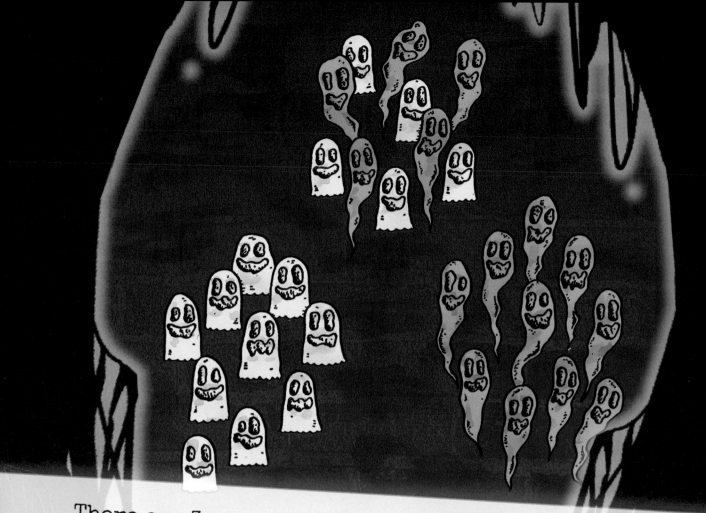

There are 3 groups of 10 ghosts, or 30 ghosts. If 10 of those ghosts disappear, how many ghosts remain? The picture will help you solve the equation.

TENS DIGIT ⌐

30 ghosts – 10 ghosts = ? ghosts

Do you need a hint? Subtracting by 10 makes the tens digit, or number, of the number you're subtracting from go down by 1.

Fifty ghosts haunt a school. Ten ghosts decide to haunt the playground instead. How many ghosts remain at the school? The picture will help you solve the problem.

$$\begin{array}{r} 50 \text{ ghosts} \\ -\ 10 \text{ ghosts} \\ \hline ?\ \text{ ghosts} \end{array}$$

Remember, subtracting by 10 makes the tens digit of the number 50 go down by 1.

Ghosts like to party in groups of 100!
Imagine 600 ghosts go to a party. When the clock strikes midnight, 100 ghosts go home early. How many ghosts are left? Subtract in your head.

Here's a hint: Subtracting by 100 makes the hundreds digit of the number you're subtracting from go down by 1.

HUNDREDS DIGIT ⌐ 600 ghosts – 100 ghosts = ? ghosts

SPOOKY SUBTRACTION TIPS

Some subtraction problems look harder than others. You can break the second number into two parts to make the equation easier to solve. Let's try it:

$$\begin{array}{r} 43 \\ -\ 7 \\ \hline ? \end{array}$$

This might be hard to do in your head. Try breaking 7 into two easier numbers: 3 and 4.

First, subtract 3 from 43.

$$43 - 3 = 40$$

Then, subtract 4.

$$40 - 4 = 36$$

Breaking it up makes subtracting in your head much easier!

You can also break the number being subtracted into tens and ones if it's two digits. Then, subtract in parts.

$$67 - 26 = ?$$

The number being subtracted is 26. Break it into tens and ones: 20 and 6.

Now, subtract from 67 in parts. First, subtract 20.

$$67 - 20 = 47$$

Then subtract 6.

$$47 - 6 = 41$$

You could also break 26 into 10, 10, and 6!

Now, try using one of the methods you've just learned to solve this equation:

$$54 - 13 = ?$$

DO YOU BELIEVE?

Almost half of all Americans believe in ghosts. More than one-third of all Canadians are believers. Many people in other countries are believers, too. So, are you?

Whether or not you think ghosts exist, picturing them in your head or drawing them on a sheet of paper can help you figure out subtraction problems—or any other kind of math equation. Ghosts may not be real, but they're really helpful! Spooky math problems are much more fun to solve with their help!

PEOPLE LOVE TO TELL GHOST STORIES AROUND CAMPFIRES!

21

GLOSSARY

celebration: a time to show happiness for an event through activities such as eating or playing music

equation: in math, a statement that two things are equal

graveyard: a place where people are buried

invisible: unable to be seen

mold: soft living matter that grows on damp or rotting things

represent: to stand for

solve: to find the answer

ANSWER KEY

page 7: 15 ghosts − 5 ghosts = 10 ghosts

page 8: 11 ghosts − 1 ghost − 2 ghosts = 8 ghosts

page 11: 20 ghosts

page 12: 40 ghosts

page 15: 500 ghosts

page 19: 41

FOR MORE INFORMATION

BOOKS

Bodden, Valerie. *Ghost Towns*. Mankato, MN: Creative Education, 2018.

Rudolph, Jessica. *Ghost Houses*. New York, NY: Bearport Publishing Company, 2017.

Williams, Zella, and Rebecca Wingard-Nelson. *Word Problems Using Addition and Subtraction*. New York, NY: Enslow Publishing, 2017.

WEBSITES

Second Grade Math
www.ixl.com/math/grade-2
Test your subtraction skills and learn more about math with these practice problems.

Second Grade Math Games
www.abcya.com/second_grade_computers.htm#numbers-cat
Play fun math games and practice your subtraction.

INDEX